# My Mommy Wears Combat Boots

by

Sharon G. McBride

*AuthorHouse™*
*1663 Liberty Drive, Suite 200*
*Bloomington, IN 47403*
*www.authorhouse.com*
*Phone: 1-800-839-8640*

*Published by AuthorHouse 09/05/2019*

*ISBN: 978-1-4343-5164-7 (sc)*

*Print information available on the last page.*

authorHOUSE®

My mommy is in the U.S. Army. She wears combat boots and a uniform to work. She said that makes me an Army baby. Because she is a soldier, sometimes the Army takes her to far away places.

That makes me feel sad, and I cry. Mommy said it's OK to feel sad. Being sad is a part of missing someone when they are not with you. I definitely miss my mommy.

When mommy is away, I stay with Grandma. My friend Tommy's mommy wears combat boots too. When his mommy goes away, he has to stay with his aunt. Mommy said I need to be good for Grandma while she is gone. Sometimes I don't want to be good for Grandma because I feel sad inside. When I am sad, it feels like my heart hurts. I just want my mommy to come home.

Sometimes I talk to mommy on the phone while she's away, and sometimes Grandma reads her e-mails to me. Mommy said she would be home as soon as she can. Grandma and I count the days off on a calendar until it's time for mommy to come home. This helps me feel better.

When Mommy is away, she said part of her job in the Army is helping other kids and babies, like me, who live far away. Mommy said these kids don't have good food to eat or shoes to wear on their feet. Mommy bought me a cool pair of shoes before she left. When I run in them, my heels light up with little flashing lights. My mommy told me to think of her and how much she loves me when I wear my cool shoes. This also helps me feel better.

Sometimes I feel mad that Mommy is far away. I can't help it. I'm mad at my mommy for leaving. It isn't fair. When I am mad, I want to yell, kick or hit something or someone. Like my Grandma or our dog. Mommy said it's OK to be mad, but it's not OK to yell, kick or hit Grandma or the dog. That will get me a time out. But it's OK to yell into or to hit my pillow - if I need to. Sometimes that makes me feel better.

My mommy said my voice is for saying, "I love you," not for yelling. She said my feet are for running and playing in the yard, not for kicking. She also said my hands are for playing with my toys, or petting our dog - nicely, not for hitting.

But sometimes I feel scared too. Like when I wake up in the middle of the night and Mommy isn't there. She used to always be there. My mommy said that is OK too. She told me when I am mad, sad or scared, I should go to my Grandma, and talk about how I feel. Grandma will give me extra kisses and hugs. That will make me fee better until my mommy comes home.

My mommy also said she loves me no matter what, and I should say a prayer for her every night before I go to bed. I should also pray for all the other Army babies, like me, who also miss their mommies. Because there are lots of mommies who wear combat boots.

Printed in the United States
By Bookmasters